WOUNDED HEALER

CHANNELING PURPOSE AND
POWER TO HEAL FROM
THE INSIDE OUT.

SHAMANDA BURSTON

WWW.13THANDJOAN.COM

Wounded Healer. Copyright © 2019 by Shamanda Burston. All rights reserved. No part of this publication may be reproduced, distributed, or transmitted in any form or by any means, including photocopying, recording, or other electronic or mechanical methods, without the prior written permission of the publisher, except in the case of brief quotations embodied in critical reviews and certain other noncommercial uses permitted by copyright law. For permission requests, write to the publisher, addressed "Attention: Permissions Coordinator," 500 N. Michigan Avenue, Suite #600, Chicago, IL 60611.

13th & Joan books may be purchased for educational, business or sales promotional use. For information, please email the Sales Department at sales@13thandjoan.com.

Printed in the U.S.A.

First Printing, June 2019

Library of Congress Cataloging-in-Publication Data has been applied for.

ISBN 978-1-7331313-2-2

TABLE OF CONTENTS

INTRODUCTION	....	1
CHAPTER 1:	Bleeding Ears & Trauma	3
CHAPTER 2:	Family Dysfunction & Addiction	.15
CHAPTER 3:	Too Young to Die…	25
CHAPTER 4:	Abuse Isn't Love	35
CHAPTER 5:	Repeating the Cycle	39
CHAPTER 6:	Single Parenting in Poverty	51
CHAPTER 7:	Breaking the Cycle	59
CHAPTER 8:	Healing	67

INTRODUCTION

What made you become a counselor? This is one of the most frequently asked questions for therapists and other mental health professionals. Daily we are tasked with helping people solve problems that are sometimes unsolvable. We are challenged with listening to heartbreaking stories of trauma, abuse, and neglect without significant emotional impact. We are asked to remain unbiased, unbothered and unchanged. Many counselors dedicate their entire professional lives to this work. Some become overwhelmed and exit due to significant burnout and compassion fatigue. As a relatively new counselor in comparison, I have found my place in this world of helping and healing. But first, I must share my story.

What is a wounded healer? By definition, a wounded healer is someone who has endured his or her own pain, survived and is now able to assist others in healing. Psychologist Carl Jung described the wounded healer-client relationship as "the doctor is effective only when he himself is affected. Only the wounded physician heals." In professional counseling relationships, self-disclosure is kept to an absolute minimum to protect the client. In my memoir, Wounded Healer, I am sharing my journey from birth to early adulthood. I have experienced and survived many of the same traumas, situations, and failures of many of my clients who sit across from me daily. In those sessions, it is the client's time and space to share; this book is my time.

It is my hope that my memoir serves as a lesson and prevention for adolescents and teenagers. For adult men and women, I hope that healing, self-forgiveness, and greater insight are the result. In the spirit of transparency, this is my most self-less act; sharing my unfiltered story with the world in hopes of providing hope that you too can overcome obstacles, challenges, abuse, and trauma. We are in this fight together. May we all heal as we give others permission to heal.

CHAPTER 1:
BLEEDING EARS & TRAUMA

When I was four years old I watched my mother's ear drip with blood.

She was standing in the bathroom curling her hair as she prepared to leave for the day. I didn't know where she was going but I sat and watched her as usual. I admired my mother's desire to look nice and decent, in fact, I was very attached to my mother. My father and I sat on the couch watching a video with photos from a recent family photo shoot. His father was a photographer and had taken those photos of us. My father and I had a strange and awkward relationship. I loved my father but I was very afraid of him. Every child should have a healthy dose of fear of their parents, at least, that's what the Bible says. However, my fear was much more exaggerated; I was terribly afraid of my father. My father was not very open and I could not randomly ask for hugs and kisses. I wanted the kind of relationship with my father that I saw on cartoons and movies. What I didn't know was that our relationship was like the movies—horror movies.

I witnessed my father hit my mother without remorse so I thought he might possibly hit me too; although he never did. As a small child, my father never hit me, he never yelled at me, he never punished me. My father gave me a whooping once when I was about eight years old. I had asked for something in the neighborhood store and somehow by asking, I disobeyed my father. That day he said, "I'm going to whoop you when I get home." I had never been so afraid of anything in my life. Anxiety and fear rushed throughout my body as I imagined the worse possible beating of my life. For years, I had heard my brothers cry out for mercy when my father would issue out their punishment. I would nervously stand by the door filled with anger and resentment. I would wish that I was brave enough to bust down the door and grab the belt from my father. My brothers did not deserve that level of punishment, I didn't understand what made him so vicious. The tougher he became and the rougher he was with my brothers the more resentful I became. That resentment quickly spread, and soon it wasn't just towards my father—I started resenting my mother too.

I could not understand how a mother would allow her sons to be beaten. Sometimes my mother would try to stop my father but it never worked. Nothing could stop him when he had his bouts of rage. While sitting on the couch that day, I watched my mom get dressed admiring her beauty. When I saw my father's eyes drift from the TV to the bathroom where my mother was my anxiety kicked in. I had become in tune with the signs that my father was about to beat my mother.

Time has a way of quickly passing when emergencies transpire. In hindsight, this argument was not about my mother curling her hair, nor was it about her leaving the house. No. The root of this argument, and the countless others, was my father's insecurities. Insecurities with infidelities that never ceased. Insecurities that birth an unhealthy jealousy. Insecurities which led to a possessiveness that transformed him into a monster. Then suddenly, with my four-year-old eyes as witnesses, they began to fight. I saw my mother leave the bathroom holding her ear. My heart stopped as I noticed blood dripping from her hand to the floor. She sat on the glass table in the living room as she called for an ambulance. My father left quickly before they arrived to escape the consequences of his actions. As a four-year-old child, I knew this was not normal. How could this be normal if it left me feeling scared, nervous, anxious, and unsafe? Moving forward I felt it was my responsibility to protect my mother—even from herself. After that event, I was no longer a child, at least I didn't feel that I could be. Someone needed to protect my mother and brothers. I had to be brave.

When my mother hurt, I hurt. Not only had I watched my father beat my mother with his hands, I had seen him emotionally abuse her too. Children learn from observation and the behaviors of their parents, and I was no exception. When I was eight-years-old, I vowed to never trust other women. I disconnected from the idea of ever having female friendships. My mother had learned several times that my father cheated. What made it worse, was that these women were her salon customers. She sat and giggled with them. She fed them as she cooked a meal for my father. She listened and gave them advice about their relationships, little did she know they were interfering with hers. She would later learn that my father had sex with 'this and that woman' and the next client. This cycle repeated itself until my mother became immune to it. Always being around my mother, I'd hear about the incidences and became just as guarded as my mother.

My mother seemed to never change her outlook or perspective of her friends. I, however, had learned that females could not be trusted. I would stare at my mother's female clients as if I was inspecting them for signs of dishonesty. For many nights, I watched my mother cry after learning that my dad sexed one of her close friends. The most bizarre situation included a female who attempted to run over my father and expose their secret relationship to my mother. Another incident, and the most hurtful, was my uncle's girlfriend informing my mother of her prior relationship with my father. She had been a sweet and kind lady. She had taken me to eat and I'd bonded with her in hopes of having a new aunt. Learning of her history with my father hurt and scarred me; probably more than it had my mother. What I didn't know at the time, was this was not new for my mother. In fact, her history of hurt was an extensive one.

My mother spent her twenties in and out of relationships. The relationships were brief and eventually I learned to not get close to the men she dated. She would always find a simple reason to end those relationships, which almost always had to do with money. Money and buying things had become my mother's coping strategies to deal with her pain. Years of abuse had taken its toll, yet my father's emotional abuse was the most damaging as it left hidden scars that became heavy weights that pained her for years.

My mother deeply desired to feel loved and appreciated. She had a father, a mother, and a family; yet, she felt empty. She was in search of a substance to fill that void— the void that every young woman is introduced to after traumatic experiences. My mother had hopes of opening a hair salon and engaging in her passion. However, in her final year of high school her dream was put on hold, when she dropped out of school while pregnant with me.

Although my mother's sisters had gotten pregnant earlier, she knew it would be frowned upon if she became pregnant too. She was the youngest child of my grandfather—a deacon at the neighborhood church. My grandfather hated the idea of others from the church judging his family and making comments regarding the babies born out of wedlock. She was seventeen and pregnant and refused to share the news with anyone. How would people view her after getting pregnant by the most popular and most wanted guy in the school? It was her first time having sex and that was all it took.

My mother's older sister ousted her to my grandparents before my mother had gotten the courage to do so herself. That day, she became so angry and outraged that she punched the living room window to prevent herself from hitting her sister. The secret was out of the bag and she had not prepared for the after effects. To make matters worse, my father was ignoring her and continued to be with other women. He was not yet ready to be a father and acknowledge his new duties. My mother was disappointed in herself and shamed by the potential comments from church folk. Surely they would shame her and look upon my grandfather as less of a man.

She decided that she needed time away from her family and time to reflect on her upcoming role as a mother. So, she departed from the family home and spent time at the local women's shelter. She stayed there for months thinking, crying, and reading. She read books aloud to me in the womb with a desire to impart a love for reading. Perhaps that is why I feel as though I have existed in other lives outside of this current life. I listened to various stories while in the womb right until the day I born. Just prior to her delivery date, my mother finally allowed my grandmother to convince her to come back home. At home, she prepared for her new life as a teenage mother and high school dropout. Prior to giving birth she bumped into an old classmate while running some errands. The classmate inquired about my name but my mother had not yet decided. She suggested that mother give me the name "Shamanda". "It's something unique, different and beautiful," her classmate said. My mother agreed and gave me that exact name.

Shortly after giving birth, my mother completed her high school diploma. Things started to look up, yet quickly took a turn when she became pregnant again. Exactly one year and three days later, my brother was born. Determined to finish, she continued her studies in cosmetology school. She worked hard, but another curveball was thrown when she learned of her third pregnancy. Once again, she dropped out.

WOUNDED HEALER

With three children, and after years of an "on-again, off-again relationship", my parents decided to get married. The physical abuse, cheating, and dysfunction continued. Within three years, my mother filed for divorce. Their marriage was a blur filled with filled with constant fights, with my mother leaving the home to escape my father's abusive hands, and me as a child attempting to make sense of it all with my innocent mind. The abuse progressed and soon she realized that we could not stay. Black trash bags still trigger flashbacks of our attempted escapes. One day when my father left for work, my mother, brothers, and I packed black trash bags full of "laundry". It was scary and nerve-wrecking. What if he came home early and saw us packing? What would he do to her? Just weeks earlier he had beat my mother in front of me. I couldn't' imagine what he would do if he saw us packing. Abuse became a normal part of my world. I learned to stay in my room to prevent being exposed to the abuse but that day I couldn't. I knew he was home when I heard my mother's screams. I ran to the living room to find my mother being choked by my father.

"Call the police Shamanda," my mother yelled out.

"You better not touch that phone or I'll whoop you," my father viciously screamed as his hands stayed wrapped around her neck. Who places an innocent child in this situation? It took me years to forgive them both for that single incident. My father had justified my mother's beating that night with the fact that she used my hair products on her clients. I made the mistake of telling my father that my mother had neglected to fix my hair. The next day, my mother looked at me with disappointment. At eight-years-old I begged my mother to forgive me for "getting her beat". Why did I need to apologize for something that wasn't my fault? At that moment, I lost respect for them both.

How do you recognize signs of trauma, abuse, and neglect in a child? One way, may be their attempt to be perfect. That was the biggest sign and clue for anyone in my life. As a child, I never got into trouble. I made it my business to be the best daughter, student, and child ever. My teachers never dealt with any issues from me. I remained to myself and pushed peers away who attempted to be my friend. I just wanted to be left alone. My teachers would inform my parents that parent teacher conferences would not be necessary; I was the top performer and most well behaved. So much so that in elementary school I was selected as a peer mediator. In hindsight, I was being shaped as a Therapist from early on.

I was a perfect child but to my own detriment. I had learned to validate myself. My mother and father spent much of their time meeting with teachers for my brothers that they often forgot about my emotional needs. My parents would brag about me to friends and family but only in comparison to my brothers negative behaviors. At times, I felt tempted to misbehave just to receive some desired attention from my parents. They were teaching me that good behavior meant being overlooked despite the unreasonable expectation to always behave well. I felt as though I was being punished for not making mistakes. The lack of attention was punishment for being a good girl, not adding to the home chaos, and for making good grades and never needing homework assistance. I was my parent's helper in every way possible. I even taught my youngest brother how to read and tie his shoes. I did anything to get their attention. I desperately *wanted* their attention. I needed their love and validation, yet it seemed I would never receive it.

Slowly, the anxiety and the depression started creeping in. My parents didn't notice my awkward behavior patterns taking form. I stopped eating out of metal utensils in the home because I thought they were filled with germs, no matter how much they were washed. I couldn't drink out of cups that had been in the sink and used by strangers in our home. Small tasks, soon became anxiety driven. Before I knew it, my dog phobia began. While sweeping one day, our new puppy found the broom I was using to be intriguing. The puppy began to lunge toward the broom as I swept. I felt my muscles tense and my heart begin to race. The dysfunctional and irrational thoughts began. "What if he bites my toes", I thought. My father sat on the couch watching college basketball not noticing the intense fear on my face. I attempted to sway the puppy away with the broom but he continued with more eagerness. I vowed that if I got away from the dog, I would never get close to any dog ever again. Since that day, I often wondered if my dad had been paying attention, would I have had a dog phobia. What if he had noticed my anxiety and instead help me pet the dog to release the pending irrational fears and thoughts. *What if?*

At school, I appeared to be a happy and normal little girl. One day during a typical day in fourth grade, my teacher came to me and pulled me aside. She asked me if I would like to be a peer mediator. I had no idea what the duties of a peer mediator consisted of but it sounded interesting. As a child, I never liked to stand out amongst the crowd. I didn't want the spotlight nor unnecessary attention. My teacher recommended me as a peer mediator based on my behavior and caring spirit with the other students. She thought that I was kind, helpful, and a good listener. The guidance counselor pulled myself and a few other chosen students into a room to explain what peer mediation required. She emphasized the importance of being fair, just, and not sharing the information learned outside of the "sessions". I was slightly nervous at the thought of having such a big responsibility. How was I supposed to help others solve their problems? Could I be effective? Why did my teacher think I would be a good peer mediator? I began to think of the numerous times in which I'd listened to my mother talk about all her life problems. I had heard her giving advice to her female cousins, nieces, and close friends. Listening to problems and issues had become second nature to me. Creating solutions and ideas of how to fix the issues became easy too. I'd ease-drop on the "adult conversations" that my mom's friends shared while she styled their hair. They always had "man problems" and couldn't seem to get it right. Although, I of course had never engaged in an intimate relationship as a child, I seemed to innately know how to make the right choice. "If a man is not treating you right and hitting you, leave!" I thought to myself. Although I heard the conversations, I was too young to know or understand the problems that were constantly discussed before me. As a teenager, I felt as though I had lived several lives before. This resonated even more because I have been listening to and analyzing problems since I was a little girl. My daddy would joke and say, "Shamanda has never been a child." With this background, I was confident I would make a great peer mediator.

WOUNDED HEALER

My first session as a peer mediator was easy. My fellow peer mediators and I convinced the two students to apologize to each other and re-establish a friendship. Compared to the issues I had analyzed at home peer mediation was a no-brainer.

Observing my parent's relationship taught me various lessons. I vowed to myself to not become the woman that my mother once was. I wanted to be strong and determined. I wanted a healthy relationship. I wanted to have a career and financial stability that was not dependent on my husband. I wanted to be loved by a man whom would never hit me nor intentionally hurt me. I wanted to live a life of freedom without struggling with children. I didn't want a man to damage my inner being. I vowed to be the exact opposite of both my parents.

CHAPTER 2:
FAMILY DYSFUNCTION & ADDICTION

I've been writing my entire life. Writing to understand my own thoughts. Writing to process my feelings. Writing because I was lonely and misunderstood. Writing because I simply did not fit in. My earliest memories of writing were in effort to escape. As early as I can remember I kept a diary. It was a small book with bright colors and a small lock and key was attached. I would write until the diary was almost full. Then one day, to my horror, I lost it. I worried about someone opening my diary and reading my inner thoughts. A part of me did not want anyone to have access to how I felt about my worldview and life circumstances. Venting on paper was my way of expressing my thoughts and feelings without hurting anyone or making things worse. My diary was my way of trying to make sense of the things I witnessed. This rang especially true in relation to my parents, particularly, my mother. I was my mother's best friend and because of her, I knew more about relationships than any young girl should know. Through her, I learned to never trust other females because they would sleep with your children's father and husband. I learned that people will gossip about you, especially family. I learned that not paying bills on time would lead to evictions and disconnected electricity. I learned that struggle was normal and a part of life. My experiences and observations created dysfunctional thinking that required unlearning. I soon realized that what I was being taught was not natural, normal, or appropriate. Knowing this, I somehow made the decision to go the opposite direction, different of everyone around me.

Every family has some level of dysfunctional communication. When I was around the age of ten, I would visit my great-grandparents with my mother. My mother enjoyed visiting her grandparents but I was afraid. Something about their house was odd and the smell was off-putting. It was also strange to me because it was big. Okay…maybe not *big* but it was the only two-story house I had ever entered. Growing up I had heard brief stories about my grandmother not having a great connection with her mother. My great-grandmother "gave" my grandmother away. She chose not to raise her first-born child but raised the five to six other children that soon followed. Why? Someone may ask. Until this day, my grandmother does not really know the reason but she assumed that her mother simply did not want her. What made her different and seemingly unlovable? As a therapist,

I can only imagine the many nights my grandmother cried herself to sleep with feelings of inadequacy and sadness. She never expressed her feelings related to her upbringing. Despite this, she managed to maintain a relationship with her siblings.

When my great-grandmother passed away I saw my grandmother cry for the first time in my entire existence. My grandmother is very stoic and unemotional. I believe that she taught herself to not cry nor express much emotion, other than anger. Because of this my grandmother raised her children to be very dependent. Her fear of losing her children and not taking care of them resulted in her creating an enmeshed family system. Throughout the family were deeply rooted issues of envy, jealousy, resentment, and discontentment. My grandmother believed that we should all be at the same level. One child should not have more than the other, no matter how hard he or she worked. She would gossip about one adult child to the other adult children. Dysfunction doesn't look odd or strange to those engaged in it. Sadly, for years my grandmother had no idea how she would affect our familial lineage.

My grandfather was a deacon at the church for over thirty years. Interestingly enough, he too had parental issues. His mother—who he never met—passed away when he was an infant leaving him with a void. He was raised by his grandmother and sparingly by his father. He has one brother whom he stayed in contact with throughout his life. His brother was rumored to be very successful and lived in New York. My grandfather would brag about his brother with pride. My grandfather worked as a custodian at the health department which drastically differed from his brother's occupation.

My grandfather was the leader of a gospel group and traveled across the USA. As a little girl, I loved music and singing. I can attribute my love for music, writing, and singing with growing up listening to my grandfather's group rehearse in the living room. My grandmother would hide out in her room as the living room was completely taken over by instruments, microphone stands and the groups mates. Listening to my grandfather rehearse filled me with a sense of pride. My grandfather was someone special; a true artist. Like my grandfather, I had a love and passion for music.

Although my grandfather was a religious man, hard-worker, and overall good father, he cheated on my grandmother. The result of his infidelity lead to the birth of my Aunt D. Her birth was a slap in the face to my grandmother and seemingly the result of a woman "not supporting her man". This left me feeling on edge with every romantic relationship. Would I be enough? If I didn't do something "right" would he leave me for another woman? My grandfather's defense was that my grandmother never supported his gospel shows, and never showed interest in his music—she wasn't present for the things that he truly loved. The mistress and mother of his out-of-marriage daughter was at every show and showed interest. In spite of his infidelities, my grandmother stayed in the marriage—making sure she brought up the details of my grandfather's infidelity every chance possible. As a child, my grandmother would stand in the kitchen fussing at my grandfather for random reasons…and whatever the reason, she would always say "Well, if you weren't paying child support we wouldn't be late," etc. I guess karma really is a bitch. They are still together by the way.

My father was a disciplinarian. I would cringe and cry whenever my brothers received whooping's. After each incident, the hostility toward my father grew. But it wasn't always this way. When my parents initially split, I was very much a "daddy's girl". I thought my father could do no wrong and that my mother was to blame for his absence. Although there was frequent fighting and arguing, I felt protected when my father was in the home. My father worked every day and unlike my mother, he ensured that the bills were paid. My mother's job was to ensure a homemade meal was prepared for dinner, clean clothes, and my hair was kept. My father was very structured, aggressive, and ego-driven. It was his way or no way at all. I have some of his character traits in which I am thankful. My desire to accomplish freedom, wealth, and nice things came from him. When I was child, my father's nickname was Mr. High Society because of his attitude and out of this world confidence. He adopted the name and even created a tag in which he placed on the front of his very first black Mercedes.

My dad was flawed, but I loved him. When he left, he took a part of me with him. What happens to women who are not raised with their fathers? All my life I searched for something to fill the void my father left. For many years, I ignored the aching desire for a secure relationship with my father. Men are providers, protectors, and maintainers of women, my father was no exception. I was searching for him in every man that I met. I needed a man that called me every day and responded immediately to my text messages. I needed protection. I desired a man that would call to ensure I had made it home safely from work and school. I needed protection. I wanted a man that would offer to assist financially and to alleviate some financial burden and stress. I needed a maintainer. I wanted a man who would show me affection with hugs, kisses on the forehead and words of encouragement. I was seeking what my father never gave me as a child. I thought I wanted a man who was possessive and jealous. I later learned that I desired that *'no you can't go out with him'* experience from my father. I wanted my father to be selective in whom he would allow me to interact with. I wanted to have a curfew, rules, guidance, long annoying talks, no sex until marriage talks. I wanted a father. I *needed* parents. Instead I had a lot of freedom.

Boys also need their fathers. Although I am a woman and my experience differs, over the years, I witnessed the decline of my brothers. My brothers and I are "stair-step children"; we are literally one year a part. I unknowingly became my mother's co-parent and was often more aware of my brother's needs than she was. Because of the abuse, having children at a young age, and feeling unfulfilled, my mother spent her twenties focused on two things: men and the club scene. For many years, my mother spent every weekend partying with friends and men. I despised her lifestyle and strongly desired for her to stay home and slow down. I watched her go from an unhappy married mother to a wild and free single mom. My brothers' and I were paying the price for her newfound freedom.

Although she ensured we had a home, the attention to our emotional needs lacked. Parenting seemed to be a burden and a curse for my mother. My father had left her with three children, an unfinished cosmetology degree, and a skewed perspective of love and relationships. Soon my brothers were failing in school and the negative behaviors increased. Every day there were issues on the bus, in the classroom, and academically with my brothers. As young boys, my brothers would confront my mother and say things such as "you're always going out and leaving us with grandma." In hindsight, they felt the same emotions as I. I never validated my brother's feelings, instead I explained to them that our mother needed time to enjoy her friends. I rationalized my mother's emotional neglect and simultaneously taught my brother's that they were wrong for desiring time and attention.

I have this deep love and respect for Black men in America. I have grown up with two Black men and watched their struggles from a close view. When boys are pre-teens, they need male mentors more than ever. As my health deteriorated and became a primary focus for my mother, my brothers became more than a handful. Because of this, in hopes of improving their behaviors, they were sent to live with my father. Unbeknownst to us, the innocent boys that left our small city of Shelby, North Carolina would not return unchanged.

It was no secret that my father was a drug dealer. He was flashy, confident, and never without money. Somehow my father had made the switch from hardworking man to the fast and easy money lifestyle. He was the supplier and provided people with money for working for him. It never made sense to me that my mother struggled so much to maintain our home when my father kept stacks of money. My brothers improved in school but were treated as servants by my father. He was a dictator; everything he requested had to be completed in a timely manner or consequences would follow. My brothers later shared that he once made them stand outside on a cold snowing day with nothing but underwear on. My father did not see anything wrong with his actions; in fact, he thought they were humorous. My oldest brother began having sex at age twelve because my father provided him with a "woman". As a result of this, and years later, he still has intimacy and relationship issues. The most scarring thing was their exposure to selling drugs as young boys. He taught them the life under the guise of "learning how to hustle and make money," so much so, that that is all they knew.

At the end of my father's stint as drug dealer, the Feds ran into his home. My brothers shared with me the fear associated with having large guns pointed in their backs. The fear of losing their lives if they made one small move paralyzed them. My brothers' were traumatized at eleven and twelve years old by those experiences. I resented my illness for being the cause of my brothers' moving with my father. I thought, it was all my fault. It took years to undo the self-blame and resentment.

For some odd reason, African-American families tend to hide things such as illness. When a person becomes sick, for example, given a Cancer diagnosis, we keep things on the "hush hush" or "the down low". Throughout my life, I have lost multiple family members whom no one knew were sick. Although this is true for physical illness, it is even more relevant when speaking of those who struggle with addictions. My family is full of addictions. My aunt Josie Mae was the most prominent family member yet she struggled with alcohol use disorder. She drank more than most men during her use period.

My maternal grandmother birthed eight children. The eldest of those was my aunt Josie Mae. Aunt Josie Mae was the go-to hairstylist in the neighborhood and could cook like no other. She only had one daughter and often vocalized her lack of desire to ever have any others due to child birth pain. Josie Mae would share stories of being chased up and down the streets "butt naked" by her daughter's father. My earliest memories of her were related to alcoholism and co-dependency. I remember multiple occasions of being awakened by her cries and begs for more money for alcohol. She would always express her feelings of lack of love and acceptance when told "no". Because my grandfather was the deacon of our hometown church for over thirty years; alcoholism, other drug use, pre-marital sex, children out of wedlock, and other sins were forbidden. Everyone knew how Josie Mae could drink and "hang". She had found healthier ways to cope with her past trauma of domestic violence and abuse. As a young girl, I didn't understand the changes that were taking place with my aunt. Suddenly I saw a different version of my aunt before me. The late-night crying, threats of running away, grabbing black trash bags to pack her clothes, images of her with glass jars with clear liquid began to disappear. The new person was happier, healthier, family-oriented, responsible, and present.

While in graduate school for Mental Health Counseling, I registered for the Substance Abuse Counseling elective class. My professor assigned an activity which included interviewing someone struggling with or in recovery from addiction. I had never heard my aunt's recovery story in its entirety and felt curious. I knew that this would be an amazing opportunity to finally pick my aunt's brain about a topic in which I was passionate about and to learn about her recovery process. One day after class, I drove to her house with my voice recorder to complete the interview. Despite cigarette smoke, various interruptions from her neighbors I gathered quite a lot of information for my assignment. A few things stood out to me the most: she was fifteen plus years sober; she had been given a prognosis of death if she ever drank alcohol again; she had pancreatitis; she attended a few AA meetings; she was currently in active counseling; and she'd experienced the "rock bottom experience" which lead to her sobriety. She shared that it was her prayers to God that delivered her from alcoholism. She spoke to me about the support she received during her initial recovery from Alcoholics Anonymous members and counselors. I knew that I wanted to be that person who helped someone regain a life of sobriety as someone helped my aunt. That day I fell in love with Mental Health and Addictions counseling.

My aunt was an amazingly beautiful person. She would "tell you off" but give you the shirt off her back. Many times, I would call her in despair, needing extra money to buy a gallon of gas to make it to class. She would give me snacks and groceries when I was close to the end of the month and low on food. Her greatest joy was her daughter Alicia and grandchildren. Jokingly, we would wish that I was her daughter and my cousin Alicia was my mother's child. Josie Mae desired that her daughter create stability in her life for herself and children. On August 14th 2014 at 1:57pm I experienced my first loss. My aunt lost the battle to Liver Cancer. I've lost several family members throughout my life but none ever pierced my soul like this loss did. It was a loss like no other. On that day I realized I needed to make significant changes in my life. It was time to live my best life.

CHAPTER 3:
TOO YOUNG TO DIE...

The smell of saline triggers memories of my illness. I still remember feeling hopeless and scared. There was a daily sense of anxiety as I awaited the next session of pain. The medications never worked and the touch from others worsened the pain. "Why me God?" I thought. "What could I have possibly done at such a young age to deserve this illness?" The doctor said there was no cure for Crohn's Disease. My first experience came while getting my hair braided. As I sat on the floor, I felt a sharp and consistent pain in my stomach. I moved and stretched in hopes that it was simply an awkward position while sitting that caused the pain.

"Take the girl to the emergency room!" my grandmother yelled instructing my mother of her next move. Thank God for southern grandmothers.

When we arrived at the hospital, I was given a tall cup of orange liquid to drink. At first glance it looked like orange soda but I wasn't that naïve. It wasn't too bad but it didn't taste great either. The doctor thought it may have been my appendix but recommended that I visit my primary care pediatrician before scheduling surgery. *Thank God!* Approximately one week later my mother and I met with my pediatrician whom diagnosed me with Crohn's Disease. Over sixteen years later, I still wonder how he knew.

He referred me to a pediatric gastrologist in Gastonia, North Carolina to begin treatment. Dr. W. Stokes Houck, MD, Pediatric Gastroenterologist is the man that saved my life! He knew how to confront me about not taking my medications without making me feel bad. I hated taking all those medications especially since I couldn't swallow pills. I was prescribed steroids for inflammation and other meds but neither controlled nor stopped the pain. Any type of foods with seeds or thick consistency resulted in severe flare ups. A flare up was five to ten minutes of hell or severe pain in my abdomen that challenged any level of labor contractions. All I could ever do was wait it out. The pain was in control and had a mind of its own. I was helpless and simply a vessel for the immune disorder to dominate and thrive.

I remember my initial colonoscopy and internal GI tract X-ray. That day, I had no idea what I was in for. The nurse led my mother and I into a small room and left me with three medium sized cups full of "barium". It looked like a vanilla milkshake, at least that is what my twelve-year-old self assumed it tasted as such. Boy, was I wrong. I took a gulp in hopes of quickly getting through the procedures. I immediately felt as though I would vomit. The thick consistency of the barium took my five senses by surprise and the taste completely shocked my taste buds. "No way!" I said as I handed the cup to my mother. "This taste like throw up. I'm not drinking this," I cried. After almost an hour and only a few sips later, my mother threatened to whoop me if I didn't drink the barium. I finally drank enough to allow the procedure. I held my nose and imagined myself drinking a tasty milkshake and it worked. It was moments like that, which triggered my depression.

    I couldn't understand why I would be dealing with the stress of surviving this painful illness after everything I had already endured. While my mother worked, I would lie on my grandparent's couch in constant pain. I would watch them watch the soap opera shows faithfully and enjoy their simple lives. Everything about my life was turned upside down. I once enjoyed riding through the city and people watching. Now, riding in a car resulted in pain every time my mother turned the car or hit a rock in the rode. I became suicidal and sometimes thought about opening the car door and "accidently" falling out while my mother was driving. I simply did not want to exist in a world with chronic pain. It was unbearable and watching other people live and enjoy their lives made me angry.

    My life consisted of monthly doctor's appointments, daily medication battles, forcing myself to eat and always checking the scale. I had always been teased for being skinny but now it was worse. I was getting smaller and weaker by the day and nothing helped. I attempted to go to school and behave like a normal preteen. I was in the eighth grade and looking forward to starting high school. My peers would stare at me and ask if I was anorexic. In health class, there was always a lesson on eating disorders and I felts eyes always shifted to me. I had the infamous spotlight effect. I'll never know if the teachers and my peers thought I was anorexic, but I do remember the embarrassing feelings associated with those moments. I often wondered if there was another type of eating disorder; the kind that consisted of eating a lot in hopes of gaining weight, if so, that was my eating disorder. Every day after school I would rush home to eat and count my calories only to be confronted with the pain associated with eating. The medications weren't working, my weight continued to decrease, and I began to develop other health complications such as arthritis. Have you ever met a thirteen-year-old with arthritis? I never knew it was possible until the doctor explained the fluid that had developed around my knee. I spent the morning in Algebra class and was excited for lunch when suddenly as I stood I felt a weight on my leg. "Why is my knee so big?" I thought. My mother picked me up from school that day and I never returned the same.

    We tried everything at this point but nothing seemed to work. Every three months I had a Remicade transfusion at the hospital to decrease inflammation in my lower bowels. I would wait at my grandparent's house after school until my mother arrived from work. We would enjoy the drive to Charlotte while listening to music and catching up on the latest gossip. I knew my mother was tired but she was all I had. By this time the doctors had attempted every possible medication and if this didn't work, surgery was the final resort.

The nurses were friendly and made sure I was comfortable throughout the medication transfusion session. For approximately three hours I would eat snacks, watch a TV show, and daydream about life after my illness while the medication flooded my veins. Many times, I would look over at my mother as she slept from exhaustion. How scary it must have been for her to watch her oldest and only daughter battle an illness. I cared about her thoughts and feelings, sometimes more than my own. Many days I would pretend to be okay but I the truth is I wanted to die. After about three transfusions within nine months, the medication was no longer effective against the immune disease. My immune system had become weaker and no longer tolerated the medication.

I was losing weight by the day and although my mother cooked full course meals for me, I could only eat a few bites. I sometimes wished that she would at least attempt to hide her dismay and frustrations. "I'm trying mom...I'm trying but I just can't eat." I thought. My feelings were passive but my words were harsh at times. "I don't want anymore," I said. I knew she'd spent an hour cooking; but, she didn't live with chronic pain and I resented her for not being more empathetic and for expecting more from me. She eventually quit her job to stay home with me full-time. At this point I had been approved for SSI disability benefits and we used that income along with other government assistance to get by.

My brothers' wellbeing was another added stressor. As my health continued to deteriorate and brothers' behaviors increasingly worsened, an agreement was created. My dad took my brothers to live in Rutherfordton, North Carolina with him while my mom was responsible for me. I worried about my brothers every day. I had spent my entire childhood caring for them and striving to be the responsible big sister. Now they were going to go live with my drug dealer of a father. My father "was the plug" in Rutherford County and everyone knew. He always had wads of money, tailored suits and shoes to match with a neck and handful of gold jewelry. He had been robbed a few times and I always worried about his safety. He had "workers and security" but with that came a lot of haters and the eyes of the DEA. I never wanted my brothers to be exposed to that lifestyle. I would lie in my mother's bed in pain with racing thoughts and lurking depression and resentment.

By this time, my mother had grown accustomed to the cries and almost entirely given up on attempting to soothe me. I resented her for spending time on the phone talking to "male friends", gossiping with her home girls and preparing for a fun filled weekend or date. "Why does her life continue? How is it fair that everyone else can enjoy their lives? Where are my grandparents, cousins, and other family members?" I thought. I had scolded my mother numerous times for telling people about my illness. I didn't like others knowing that I was sick. I was in denial and comforted by not acknowledging my reality. My mother often spoke to others about my illness with a desire for sympathy. I resented her for that too. "Why does it matter how this affects you? You are not the person in constant pain" I thought. In hindsight, I was in the anger stage of grief. It was hard for her too. After all, who wants to watch their daughter wither away and die? My mother was in her early thirties and still seeking freedom. Like her, I carried many resentments. I blamed her and my father for my illness once I learned that stress is a trigger. How does one develop Crohn's Disease? Genetics and Stress. Stress from years of exposure to my parent's domestic violence, worrying about how we'd pay the bills, staying up late waiting for my mother to come home from the club, worrying about my brothers, and knowing too much about life problems as a young girl. It was their fault!

My lowest weight was fifty-five pounds. I had become so weak and fragile that I looked like someone's elderly grandmother hunched over from years of labor and arthritis. That was my reality as a thirteen-year-old. My doctor advised that it was time to consider surgery due to my current condition and being malnourished. His suggestion came more as a warning as he would give me an ultimatum: surgery or death. How the hell was I supposed to make that decision as a thirteen-year-old? My mother said, "It's your choice." At that moment, I had all but completely given up. I was receiving my school assignments and met weekly with a teacher in my home. Despite all that was going on, I was passing my assignments with ease.

One day I asked myself if I wanted to live and why? As I reflected on my life, a Joel Osteen segment appeared on TV. My mother had left to shop at Goodwill so I was alone with the TV, once again. Moments earlier I had asked God for direction and revelation regarding the pending surgery. I bear witness that God answers prayers! Joel Osteen's message was in direct response to my prayer. I immediately began to cry and beg God for forgiveness. I thanked God for sparing me over the past year and for the strength that he had provided. I asked God to forgive me for the harshness of my tongue, to heal me from the resentment I harbored toward my parents and family, and prayed for the strength as I moved forward. Immediately God showed me my future and all the many reason I had to live. There was a purpose and it was much greater than me. It wasn't my time to leave this world. God showed me the spotlight on a stage in which I had dreamt about as a child. God revealed that thirteen was not the end of my life. God said, "Greater is coming…this is simply part of your story." I cried. I cried and cried until I fell asleep on the living room couch.

I was awakened by the doorbell. "Who could that be", I thought. Hours earlier my father had called and asked about the surgery. I'd told him that I didn't know if I wanted to live or die yet. I opened the door and to my surprise stood my father and uncle. Although my father was never a super religious man, he prayed with me that day. I cried even more as I once again declared my desire and will to live. In three hours, my life was changed forever.

After a month of walking around with a PICC line to allow IV-feedings and an assigned food journal, I was ready to go. My doctor required me to gain some weight to prevent complications from the upcoming surgery which would also help to increase my ability to fight off any potential infections. In one month, I had increased my weight from 55lbs to 70lbs with the help of my home health nurse Glenda. On my last day of treatment, she encouraged me to not be a big baby and assured me that I'd be okay. She gave me a big hug after removing my PICC line from my feeding bag. I stayed in the hospital for six days after

Laparoscopic Surgery to remove fourteen inches of damaged ulcerated small intestines. The doctors informed me that after I ate a full meal and regained the ability to have a bowel movement, I could leave. After my surgery, I gained weight fast! For the first time in my life I weighed 90 pounds. I was so happy and confident. I loved the new me! Everywhere I went people would compliment me on how healthy I looked. The guys who'd teased me all those years would ask me for my number and dates. I was finally ready to live my life as a normal teenager. I prayed to God that the disease would not return. I also prayed for humility. I had been at my worst and lowest, and I never wanted to return. Although my doctors said that a follow-up surgery might be needed within five years, I rebuked that idea. God had shown me that I had a purpose. I was ready to fulfill it.

CHAPTER 4:
ABUSE ISN'T LOVE

I've spent my entire twenties looking for him. I had this image in my mind but he doesn't have a face. He is gentle, kind and sweet. Successful, loving, and romantic. Strong, sensitive, and passionate. Spontaneous, sensuous, and patient. He is respectful, caring, and forgiving. He is selfless, intelligent, and wise. He is attractive, healthy and nurturing. He is easy-going, direct, and sarcastic. He is funny, possessive, and serious. He is every man I've bypassed for the jerks that I dated. He is the guy who likes and comments on my every photo as I pray that Mr. popular notices it. Yes, I do it too. I've given every guy a chance except the right guy. I've met him too, several times. He's in the shadow but in plain sight.

Where do we learn these dysfunctional dating patterns? Most importantly, how do we unlearn them? As a young girl, I would see other young girls walking around pregnant and scared. I remember passing them and thinking "Their lives are ruined now. How will she ever enjoy life with a baby at such a young age?" I heard all the stories of women wishing and praying that they could undo their self-professed "dumb decisions". There were the women, many whom were my mother's friends, who struggled to pay their bills, chased their "baby daddies" around the city, and fought other women who were the next victims of their "baby daddies". I had absolutely no desire to be a part of that club. Through observation I knew that life was hard and depressing. My mother's friends were always calling and asking for advice, asking to receive my gently worn clothes, and most frequently…to go out to clubs. I didn't want that for myself….

Ironically, a few years later I found myself in a very similar situation. Abuse can sometimes be disguised as jealousy and possessiveness. Females desire to feel protected, loved, and desired by their man, sometimes to their own detriment. I don't remember the first time he hit me. I would like to think that I confronted him with an ultimatum of leaving if it continued. I remember feeling stuck, scared and alone—mostly, unprotected.

Shortly after giving birth to my son I decided to have a photoshoot. After I received the photos, I noticed something about the woman in the photos. In the photo was a young woman striving to hold on to the last remnants of her old life. Also, in the photo was a bruise on the model's arm. Days before, I said something that he did not like. As a result, he punched me on the arm. I didn't notice the bruise until the day of the photoshoot. By then, it was too late; I couldn't hide it. My photographer seemed a little uncomfortable as though he wanted to ask but didn't know the words to use. Years later my photographer and I discussed the photoshoot and how he was challenged to remain calm and reserved after noticing the bruise. He was there too; holding the baby as I modeled and continued my dream. This drove him insane. I could always feel the resentment, anger, and jealousy he felt toward me. He never punched me in the face until I was bloody; no, his abuse was different. He would slap me mid-sentence. He would push me up the stairs with a belly full of baby as I tripped over each step. He would pick me up by my shirt, hold me to the ceiling, and allow my body to fall to the ground. He would force me in the car and drive 140 mph until I begged him with tears to stop. He would put a gun to my head and pull the trigger…after showing me the bullets in the chamber. He would call me 'skinny' and cheat with thick women creating a deeper dislike for self. Yes, his abuse was different. It was the kind that lingers internally and requires years of recovery. It was the kind that is undercover because there are no bruises and scars to show for it. It was the kind that causes you to question your ability to make sound decisions. It was the kind that leaves you resentful, angry and numb. I hated this *lack* of a man for years. It was only the fact, that the two beautiful beings whom I love, shared his blood, that saved my soul.

CHAPTER 5: REPEATING THE CYCLE

Sometimes we forget that our parents had lives before us. It is worth exploring the challenges they have faced which shaped their very being. Who raised you? Was it the young and inexperienced teenager or the resolved, mature and stable forty-five-year-old? We blame our parents for everything and hold ourselves accountable for little. It is not until, we ourselves grow wiser, that we realize we can learn from their mistakes. We don't have to repeat the cycle.

During graduate school I thoroughly enjoyed studying and learning about developmental psychology. Sometimes, we need to be saved from ourselves. Everything that looks good isn't good for us. *How do we protect ourselves from repeating cycles that we did not begin?* In hindsight, I repeated my mother's cycle. We dropped out of school at the same age, returned to school, experienced domestic violence, ridicule and more—all at the same age. My mother must have noticed the similarities also. A few months after I birth my daughter, she cut me with her words saying "you will get pregnant again." Tears of anger, disappointment, betrayal, and frustration fell down my face. Was my mother really hoping that I continued to fail myself? Was she envious that I had "learned my lesson" after my second child instead of three as she did? Was she giving me a dose of reverse psychology with the hopes that I work hard to prove her wrong? I don't know what her intentions were, but it hurt. I felt as though she wanted me to fail and to share this dysfunctional connection with her.

I became a mother shortly after my eighteenth birthday. I spent the month after my birthday lying in a hospital bed in preterm labor with an erupted amniotic sac. While walking to the kitchen I noticed fluid leaking between my legs. Immediately I called for my mother but remembered that she had left for a night out and had not yet returned. I frantically called my aunt Josie Mae and she quickly made her way to my mother's home to help me. The ambulance transported me to the local hospital where I was told of my preterm labor. My mother arrived to the hospital and drove me to Charlotte, North Carolina where I received all my medical care due to my high-risk status. I was scared. I was only twenty-nine weeks pregnant and my baby was underdeveloped. My doctor informed me of the plan to induce my labor at thirty-four weeks if we could stall labor for five more weeks. I was awakened at four AM for steroid shots for the baby in order to strengthen his lungs and increase his chances of survival upon induction. I had to be brave for my baby boy. I was not prepared for any of this!

After becoming a mother, I realized that we lose a part of ourselves when we become mothers at a young age. I lost my ability to explore life freely, without responsibilities. I lost my ability to sleep in late without the constant thought of "wait, where's my child?" I have no idea how it feels to date a man without assessing him for father figure qualities. I've never experienced a payday that is not focused on paying bills, food, and other necessities just for me. I cannot simply spend my money or splurge on a vacation at the Bahamas. My life has not been the same since becoming a parent.

Some people plan to have children and wisely prepare for the responsibilities to come. Growing up in my small town, being a planned parent was rarely the case. I remember being a teenager and seeing young girls in my town with big bellies and barely out of middle school. I vowed silently to not allow myself to go down that path. What is to become of someone who loses their life so early due to teenage parenting. The girls that I saw struggled with parenting and barely survived on food stamps and other government assistance. I did not want to become those girls. During my high school years, there were star athletes and other "stand outs" who were poised to make it out of our small town successfully or at least, without babies. I would always experience a sense of disappointment after learning that they were now pregnant by the neighborhood drug dealer or decided to settle down instead of pursuing lifelong dreams. I saw it all and created my own judgments. I soon learned that life has a way of "putting us in someone else's shoes."

How could the black girl in the advanced placement and honor courses become a statistic? In high school, I was the nerdy girl that both the popular kids and the overachievers liked. I could adapt with both crowds and never felt nor desired to fit in with either. I felt a sense of sorrow for the popular kids as I somehow sensed that it was all an illusion. I studied my white counterparts and how they seemed to magically balance a focus on being "cool" and maintaining grades for Ivy League Universities with SAT scores to match. My black peers steered clear of the more challenging classes but applauded me for my brevity. I was quiet and shy throughout my high school years. I spent most of my day people watching in an attempt to understand those around me. I needed friends and peers who I could relate to but it felt impossible. Would they relate to a girl who barely escaped death only a few years prior? I didn't think they would understand my struggles and my intense curiosity with people and human behavior.

I should have made friends and remained more open. I knew that some of the kids were having sex but I was too afraid. I spent my afternoons reading books, watching lifetime movies, and listening to adults share the various dramas in their lives. Socially, my brothers were drastically different from me. They would always make new friends quickly whenever we moved to a new home throughout the city. Many times, my brothers would invite their friends into our home and introduce me as their big sister. I was off limits and not attracted to my little brothers' friends. I was on track to graduate from high school after several years of challenges; no distractions were needed. Modeling was the only thing that interested me outside of school and learning. I was focused.

Do opposites attract or are we simply curious beings? I'll never forget the day that I met my children's father. He was a dark-skinned guy with a weird but interesting accent. When I first met him, he looked familiar. It was as if I met him during one of my brothers routine brief introductions of 'new friends'. I had seen this guy at a local party a few months ago. I rarely ever hung out but I was invited by a friend and could not say no. What was interesting about his guy? He shared that he was originally from Jamaica but had lived in New York, Atlanta, and Fort Lauderdale. He was a bad boy and I was a sweet and nerdy girl. I was a country girl living in the small city. He was Caribbean with a city vibe. We were both Scorpios. Soon, I was hooked. I skipped school to hang out with my drop-out boyfriend. Sex became our primary pastime. He cheated, we fought, broke up and the cycle repeated itself. That summer changed my life forever.

We like to believe that we know those whom we claim to love, but how much do we really know those that we love? At sixteen I was stuck in a domestically violent relationship. I had sworn that I would never repeat my mother and father's life, but it was happening. My deep desire to experience love and protection was the attracting factor. Although I was being pushed, slapped, dropped, punched and more, I felt stuck. I could not tell my mother about my secretly abusive relationship because she was busy being young. My mother and I had become best friends and it was never an issue until I needed a mother. Who could help me find myself as a young woman without judging my desire to be free? My father was a ghost who randomly appeared upon request…sometimes. I was lost, helpless, fearful and lonely.

In my mother's defense, I was an exceptionally smart girl. I taught more than I ever learned from those who were supposed to teach me. My mother taught me how to use a tampon but we never discussed condoms, having sex, birth control or anything of that sort. I think she simply believed that I "knew better". One day a crazy thought crossed my mind. Could I be pregnant? I had not had a menstrual cycle in over four months but was too busy to notice. What could possible explain the sudden lapse in my menstrual cycle? I was not on birth control and rarely were condoms worn with my boyfriend. I could be pregnant! I informed him of my missed cycles and the need for a pregnancy test. I took the home test that showed a positive result. In shock and disbelief, I decided to have a "real" test at the local health department the following day. My children's father and I looked at each other without a clue of what to do. Abortion nor adoption were never discussed. My greatest fear was informing my mother, who I feared would be greatly disappointed. I called my grandmother with tears and informed her of my burdensome news. I was not excited but fully afraid. I asked her to call my mother to tell her before she came home from work. The night before I had mopped around the house seeking the words to disclose my new secret. I walked in and out of the bathroom as my mother prepped her hair. I could not find the words. She was going to be a grandmother.

I began my prenatal care approximately three months into my pregnancy. Due to my digestive disease, previous surgery, and short cervix, I was considered high risk. The doctors informed me that I would need to begin bedrest as my pregnancy progressed. The stress and physical abuse continued. The possessiveness and control increased. He knew that I would be in his life in some capacity for at least eighteen years, and I quickly realized that I would become a single mother.

Approximately six months into my pregnancy, I was restricted to bedrest due to pre-term labor. My short cervix created an increased risk for an early birth. My life was spiraling downhill fast and I was no longer in control. My children's father was now incarcerated after several charges and detained for potential deportation. How much more could I take! My son would potentially never see his father if he was sent back to Jamaica. I was scared, nervous and unprepared. I wasn't ready to become a mother yet. Months prior I had come close to having an abortion. The physical and emotional abuse had worsen. I could not imagine spending my entire life running and dodging the abuse. Maybe if I didn't have his child he would finally leave and allow my freedom again. I felt helpless, depressed, and hopeless.

After five long weeks in the hospital; I delivered a beautiful baby boy at 34 weeks. The moment my son looked me in my eyes, I cried. I knew that my life had changed forever and the old me was non-existent. I had something to live and fight for. I briefly grieved the loss of the things I never experienced. I was a statistic. A high-school dropout and teenage mother. I had become those girls that I silently judged. I had repeated my mother's cycle of a domestic violence victim and single mother. Something would have to change.

My children's father was detained for over three months. I soon learned that while I was writing letters to comfort him from my hospital bed, he was making calls to other females from prison. I was hurt and embarrassed. He came home shortly after I gave birth, although our son was still in the NICU. I visited my son daily to breastfeed and to ensure our bond. I was disappointed and shocked when my children's father neglected to join me at the hospital on numerous occasions. Perhaps he was not ready to be a father, but that wasn't an excuse, as I was not prepared to be a mother either.

I experienced the pressure of attempting to find a place to live for my infant son and I. I was newly eighteen with little work experience. I had a monthly SSI check from my digestive disease and a few pay stubs from working as a promo model. I needed to find a secure and safe environment for us before he was released from the hospital. After three weeks and growing from 4 pounds, 2 ounces to 12 pounds, I was finally able to bring my baby home. Home was my mother's house where my two teenage brothers also lived. Due to receiving monthly income, my mother was okay with my living there and assisting with expenses. However, this soon became an issue as I desired to save money to rent a home and to buy my son clothing and other needs. I would have to move soon due to increased arguments and animosity between my mother and I.

My children's father and I soon realized that it would not work after less than two years. He held on to hope at times but when my son was approximately three months, I was over it. My brothers had introduced me to another friend. This guy was drastically different from my son's father. He was in school working toward his GED, working full-time at a good job and taking care of his teenage brother after their mother died. He knew of my son's father and did not appear to be threatened. I was not interested in dating and resisted his every attempt to talk to me. Slowly he grew on me and I realized we had a lot in common. He did not judge me for having a son and seemed genuinely interested in getting to know me as a woman. He took me on actual dates and treated me with respect and love. He was different and I could feel it. My son's father quickly learned of my new friendship and attempted to interfere. He threatened me and assaulted me with a knife. He sat with a knife pressed against my thigh as he forced me to inform my new friend that we could no longer see each other. Afterwards, he lifted me by my shirt and held me as he informed me of all the things he would do if I engaged with another man. On that day, he lifted my body to the ceiling and dropped me before walking out of my mother's home. I felt helpless and unsafe.

Things were not improving in the current environment. I was becoming depressed and felt stuck, again. I was eighteen, with a new baby, and no education. I had even lost a guy who truly respected me. My son's father came to the house less and less as time passed by. My mother and I would argue more frequently and I often felt that she loathed my choices and our presence in her home. Out of desperation, I informed my son's father that I needed help securing an apartment. He suggested that I move in with him and his father until I could save for a security deposit and first month's rent. I was booking several promo modeling event assignments and would soon have the money needed. Against my better judgment, I accepted his offer. I felt that his father's presence would serve as a layer of protection against the domestic violence. He respected his father and would not mistreat me...so I thought.

I made it clear from the beginning that I was simply a roommate in the home. I had absolutely no desire to engage in any type of relationship with my son's father. Our son slept in the middle of the bed as a divider. Many nights he came home at midnight to find me unbothered and careless. I was focused on my goal of finding a home, being a mother, securing a job and finishing my education. My friend and I had connected and were texting each other throughout the day. I felt alone most of the day but having his friendship gave me hope. One night my son's father came home after a long day out and about. I was sure that he was involved with someone but I was not concerned. There were many times he would try to engage in sexual activity but I would quickly turn him down and remind him of our new relationship: roommates and co-parents. The lack of control triggered his anger. His muscles became tense as he would transform into someone else. It was not uncommon for him to pin me down and penetrate me against my desire. In fact, it was far too common. I felt defenseless—afraid that he would hurt me if I forcefully fought him off. My right cheek became intimate with his left palm, imprints of his fingers left on my face silencing my no's. The weight of his hands crippled me, leaving me only with the strength to pray it would stop. And when my prayers came were unheard, my life reflected back as I became lost in the muzzle—trigger sounds as my final soundtrack. I was afraid of him. Those episodes triggered memories of my parent's physical altercations and the helpless feeling remained. I remember looking up from my book as he walked into the room. The look in his eyes were all too familiar. I quickly reminded him that I was not having sex with him and of our agreement to focus on our son and securing a home. He walked over to my side of the bed and although I pushed and kicked, it happened. Years later people ask me why I had two children with a man who was abusive. The strong and resilient woman that I had become struggled with formulating the words: I was raped.

My beautiful son and daughter are the results of two years of hell. At the age of nineteen I was a high school dropout with two children, under two-years-old. I had failed myself and disappointed so many people. I was determined to create a better life for my children and to overcome those obstacles. God has a way of turning tragedy, struggle, and pain into a wonderful testimony. I look at my children today and know that they were meant to be here. They are divinely a part of my story and life purpose. I would have never thought that I would become one of "those girls" who I focused so hard on not becoming. I never thought I'd repeat my mother's cycle, but I did. My greatest desire is to continuously heal from my experiences while helping young girls avoid them.

CHAPTER 6:
SINGLE PARENTING IN POVERTY

At eighteen-years-old, I wasn't ready to be a mother. I played with fire and got burnt the first time. I accepted the fate and felt able to handle one child. I would find a job, finish my high school diploma and create a good life for my son and I. But two children under the age of two was too much! The stares, the whispers, the judgmental comments, the loneliness, the feeling of failure; it was too much. Living everyday with the secret of how my daughter was conceived ate away at me. I was all alone and left with the responsibility to both nurture and provide for two small children and myself. My ego and pride slowly began to fade away as I applied for government assistance for food, housing, and childcare. Everything I received or earned went to the children. It was never enough. We were merely surviving as the reality of single parenting in poverty became my standard of living.

Poverty makes me nauseous. The memories of scraping pennies and dimes, searching underneath the couch cushion and car seats for loose change, looking inside purses hoping to find enough to make a dollar for gas or food, made me nauseous. All my money was applied to home expenses. Very rarely did I buy myself anything new. I'd pay the light bill, the rent for the month, the car payment and insurance, and save ten dollars for gas in hopes that it would last for the week. I always kept a budget because living on less than $2,000 a month with two growing children required me to do so. I remember the feelings of hopelessness and the dark cloud of depression. "Damnit, I don't want to live like this!", I would think to myself. At night, I would put my children to bed and sit with myself and cry. "Every day is struggle! Why is this so hard? How does he get to enjoy the freedom to come and go, to travel, to drive around in luxury cars, to live! It's not fair! I didn't ask for this and I shouldn't have to do this alone. Why me God?"

Despite my troubles, my natural ambitious spirit and desire for more out of life never left me. Although I was nineteen with two children under age two, I refused to give up. I had to create an escape plan. Poverty, single-parenting, and struggle were normal, but I didn't want to keep it a part of my reality. I needed to create a different life for us. The idea of remaining in roach infested apartments, scraping nickels and dimes for gas, depending on food stamps to feed my children, fearful of losing the housing voucher resulting in homelessness was unbearable. I had witnessed many people in my life live this type of life filled with hopelessness. I needed and desired more for myself and children. These realities were going to be short-lived. I began to read personal finance books daily. What were the people in the "Middle-Class" doing differently and how could I get there? How could I be like the women in the grocery store who paid for their grocery in cash and carried lists of items needed instead of throwing anything into the cart? How could I own a home or drive a Mercedes? What did I need to do to change my standard of living? The belief that I could change my life circumstances was scarier than attempting to do so. What would my family think of me if I declined living on government resources, graduated from college, and simply wanted more than our normal? I would become an outsider; they'd think I thought I was "all of that" and "too good". I didn't care. I looked at my children and simply decided that we deserved more and I would break the curse of poverty!

Returning to school with two small children was not easy. I'd realized that the Middle-Class were educated and if I wanted to elevate to that level, I needed to complete my high school diploma and begin college. At the time, I received less that $500 SSI disability check, a $236 work-first check from social services, and was wait-listed for a housing and daycare voucher. I didn't have a car nor childcare. I would need someone to babysit and a reliable way to school. I called the local community college and scheduled a placement test. I had one week to figure out transportation and childcare. My mother and I had gotten into an argument earlier in the week. She'd said, "You're going to end up pregnant again, watch!" My blood boiled with rage and resentment. Why would she speak those words over my life when I was attempting to care for the children I had? Why did she want me to fail? And why didn't she believe in me? I'd learned how to channel my anger toward others as fuel and motivation. I would prove her wrong by not getting pregnant again, completing my high school diploma and graduating from college.

Three months after taking my placement test I completed my adult high school diploma. I immediately registered for college courses. I chose Pre-Psychology and Business Administration as my two majors. I had no idea of what my career would be but I had faith that I would figure it out. Over the previous six months I had learned that things seemed to work themselves out when I stepped out of faith. My mother agreed to babysit the children three days out of the week as I completed my high school courses and she would let me drive the Oldsmobile to school. My sense of pride escaped me after driving the huge yellow car to school with rope tied to the trunk to stop it from swinging open. My mother never let me drive her Lexus to class. I remembered her hurtful words as I walked past her car and jumped into the Oldsmobile. I refused to give up or give in. My children deserved more and I was focused on making it happen. As the Spring semester approached, I watched God begin to open more doors to help me achieve my goals. After being on the childcare voucher for almost one year, I received notice that I was now approved for childcare assistance. After driving the "big yellow car with the flapping trunk" I found a black Lexus that I could afford with the salary from the seasonal full-time job at BELK. Everything was beginning to work out as planned.

I graduated with my adult high school diploma the same month that I completed my first semester of college as a double-major and Senator in the Student Government Association! I began to master the art of multi-tasking and time management. When I wasn't working, I was volunteering or participating in leadership activities on campus. I was elected Vice-President of Student Government and attended conferences with young college leaders from across North Carolina. In those instances, I'd have to ask my mother to babysit so I could "live a little". I'd never "hangout" just for fun because I knew my opportunities to leave my children with my mom were limited and had to be spaced out.

Each semester passed and I seemed to get closer to this life that felt unreal. I had no one to share my dreams and aspirations with. I had become the first person in my family to graduate from college. My Undergraduate graduation ceremony took place only fifteen minutes from my grandparent's house, yet, they did not attend nor did my brothers, aunts, cousins, father, siblings or uncles. Their absence left me feeling unsupported and numb. It confirmed my feelings of isolation. My mom came to assist me with the children, otherwise they would have had to walk across the stage with me. Three graduation ceremonies and almost zero family support and attendance.

I worked from 8am to 4pm Monday through Friday, attended graduate school two evenings per week, and raised two children throughout the process. Saturday mornings were allotted for study sessions. I would turn the TV channel to the children's favorite cartoons as I transcribed counseling sessions or wrote ten-page research papers for my graduate level classes. My days consisted of work, school, pick-up children from daycare, homework, sleep and repeat. My life revolved around completing my education to obtain a career that freed my children and I from poverty. The family drama whirled around me like a tornado. I'd learned to focus on myself and children with tunnel vision. My brothers were in and out of prison and jail, inconsistent communication with my father, short-lived romantic relationships, lack of support from family, no child support, even death did not distract me. I was laser-focused on my goals. The chaos, poverty, and dysfunction around me fueled my drive. "If I give up this will be my life forever. Keep going! Don't give up! Relationships and love can wait. Say "No" to mom because the kids need new shoes. Don't get mad because he's not helping. One day you won't need his help. No, you cannot send him money in jail. He had to choose a different lifestyle. Keep going! Stay focused! Almost there!", I thought to myself.

My first counseling offer came shortly after graduating with my Masters. They offered me $40,000! I had spent the past six months completing my clinical internships and practicums while surviving solely on the student loan refund checks from Summer and Fall semesters. I'd been laid off my full-time job just in time before clinicals but the money was needed. I had to make sacrifices with my budget due to severely limited funds. My dean approved my application to double my credit hours allowing me to graduate one year early! I'd managed to maintain an A/B honor roll while working full-time. My aunt had passed away a few months earlier but I didn't have time to breathe nor grieve. I had to finish this program and get to work fast. My car payment was three months behind and approaching four. I dodged calls debt collectors daily while applying for jobs and completing my application for professional counseling licensure. Multiple applications were submitted but I accepted the position in a Methadone clinic at $40,000 with full healthcare benefits and more. Our lives were about to change, finally!

From my experiences in life, there is always a storm before I see the rainbow. The next morning, I was awakened by a knock on the door at 3am in the morning. My car was being repossessed due to non-payment. My heart felt crushed by despair and the dark cloud replaced my feelings of happiness, achievement, and hope for our future. How would I start my new job without a car? I called my father but he gave me motivation without money. My pride wouldn't allow me to call my mother; although, I knew that she could not financially assist me anyway. I called my children's father but he suggested I apply for a personal loan and gave me names of such companies. Finally, I called the only person I've ever called "Friend". He transferred $1300 into my bank account immediately. I paid him back in installment payments the following month. I learned a valuable lesson that day, I am my only backup plan. The feeling of having no one to depend on was confirmed and validated that day. Having to create a false story for my children when asked "where's the car mommy?", was more than enough motivation for me. That day I committed myself to living frugally, saving, paying off debts, and taking care of my children and I first. I committed myself to breaking the cycle of poverty in our lives.

CHAPTER 7: BREAKING THE CYCLE

How does one break away from that which they've always known? As a child, I recognized that something didn't feel "right". No, I wasn't beaten, molested, nor neglected but I was lacking in many areas. The emptiness of feeling alone in my desire to achieve more, to be more, and to not struggle isolated me from my family. The reality of being different increased my sense of loneliness.

For as long as I can remember, my family utilized the government assistance program. Although my grandfather worked daily at the health department as a janitor and my grandmother in a factory, money was always an issue. My grandfather used his money to pay the household bills and to supplement my aunt's home expenses. She had a housing voucher, food stamps, and even utilities stipend but still received his financial assistance. My uncles lived with my grandparents, moving in and out periodically, always returning "home" when things were tight financially. My grandmother was the go to person when someone in the family needed a loan to pay their light bill, bail out of jail, prevent an eviction or repossession of car, gas money for work and of course, food. For many years, I watched my relatives beg my grandmother for money. At this point she was retired and received a monthly retirement and social security check. Like clockwork aunts, uncles, and cousins would make their way to my grandparent's home on the first and third of every month, always with financial requests. I witnessed this for many years into adulthood; always knowing something about this wasn't right. I would observe my grandmother's gestures and affect as she repeatedly said "No, I don't have it. I have to pay my bills." The pleading continued with an almost unconscious lack of consideration for her needs and desires. My grandmother gave in always and I sensed the energy of defeat in the room. After they'd left she would mumble to herself about what she had planned to buy herself with the money she gave out. The new sofa would have to wait, repairing the heating unit was on pause for yet another month and no, she wouldn't be able to buy herself anything.

    Co-dependency, dependency, and enabling took hold of my family like a snake does its prey. My grandparents created the environment for adult children who knew little about self-sufficiency. The unspoken desire was that the adult children remain close to home with no expectations ...just stay close. *How did this manifest?* Almost all eight of my grandparents' children struggle with some form of addiction. *What were they trying to cope with or was it hereditary?* I later learned two important pieces of information about my grandparents; both struggled with Alcoholism in their twenties and both were separated from their mothers and raised by their grandmothers during early childhood. The curse of striving to fill a void handicapped my family.

Early on I realized that I needed to do something different. I hated the feeling of constantly worrying about my mother not paying the rent on time, skipping a car payment or coming home to no utilities. Most adults attempt to shield children from those experiences; I was well aware. As my mother sought after much needed money to pay the bills, I too brainstormed potential lenders for the month. Unaware of my displacement, I felt it was my responsibility as the oldest child to worry and stress about bills and any other concern of my mothers. I was her best-friend and she was mine. As I grew older, I realized that our relationship wasn't healthy and not mutually beneficial. I had come to believe that it was my job to help take care of my brothers (i.e babysit when she needed a night out with the girls, help with the homework, and follow them around to ensure their safety). For her, my duty was to listen as she expressed her emotions. I was allowed to give suggestions and when she did not approve she'd say "stay in a child's place". I was confused! What does a child do? As early as age seven, I stopped playing with my Barbie dolls to become my mother's confidant. She needed me. Her friends were all disloyal and betrayed her by sleeping with my father, per her report. And I'd learned to not get too involved in my play in case I had to intervene when my mother and father fought.

The girls at school spoke often of their plans for college. They were sure of their scholarships for being outstanding athletes. I was a smart honors student with a social awkwardness and minimum friends. The discussion of college never came up in my home. I would secretly listen in the bathroom stall as the star basketball players spoke about their plans for college. Many of them had plans of moving far away while others would stay close to home. I was lost and unaware. My teacher assigned career assessment for each student to complete. My results: A career as a Psychologist! After reading the job description, I realized that I had been doing this work all my life. I had grown comfortable with listening, analyzing, suggesting and advising. I quickly remembered my duty as peer mediator in elementary school. To become a psychologist, I would have to finish my high school diploma, go to college, and graduate school. I can do this. "This is my purpose," I thought to myself. A few months later my knee swelled from arthritis while at school. My Crohn's disease medication was no longer effective. I would have to be homeschooled and prepare for surgery. I left school with sense of purpose and an idea of what I could do with my life. Although there was no one to talk to, I kept it reserved in my mind.

I graduated in May 2009 with my high school diploma; May 2012 with a Bachelor of Science degree and December 2014 with a Master of Arts/Education Specialist degree. Although the graduation ceremonies were less than thirty minutes from my grandparent's home, they did not attend neither of them. Resentment set in as I realized that my grandparents attended birthday parties and even gifted my brothers with money upon release from prison, but for me they never showed up. My grandparents never made it past primary school. I was the first person in the family to graduate with college degrees and yet they never showed up. I quickly learned to stop expecting support from others. Expectations of my family was setup for emotional pain and failure. I would have to be okay with walking the journey alone.

My children gave me the extra push I needed to break the cycle. If I was a young single woman without responsibilities, I would have settled. The day I brought my daughter home from the hospital, I quickly realized that there were now two children depending on me to survive. I thought about their lives as teenagers and young adults. I wanted to do everything differently from how I was raised. I wanted to provide them with a financial head start in life. I wanted them to make life decisions based on passion, talent, and skills rather than need for money to survive. I wanted to expose them to different communities, cultures, and a higher standard of living. I wanted to show them that although we were starting from the bottom, hard work, sacrifices and determination would allow us to soar. I wanted to show them that love, support, and encouragement were natural elements of family and freely given. I wanted to shield them from traumatic experiences, stress related to bills, and poverty. Breaking the cycle would have to begin with my children.

Radical changes require radical choices and actions. I decided to create a different life for myself and children. I had no clear idea of how our lives would look so I began to research. The concept of "Middle-Class" was somewhat foreign to me. I'd seen those words in magazines, heard them in my classes and even read them in books and articles. I needed to quickly answer two questions: What is Middle Class? and How do I transition from poverty/lower-class to Middle-Class? I began to spend hours in between school and work inside the library reading about personal finance. Suzy Orman, Napolian Hill, "Think and Grow Rich", "Rich Dad, Poor Dad", "Millionaire Next Door" and more. As I read, my mindset began to shift. The poverty mindset was being replaced with a wealth mentality. Life was no longer about surviving and suddenly I wanted to thrive. Life wasn't about having enough money to pay bills for the month but having more to save for retirement, pay for my children's college expenses, pay my rent without government vouchers, pay cash for grocery instead of food stamps, pay childcare and medical expenses without government assistance, enjoying my work as a career and not simply a job. There was a whole class of people who didn't live like we were living. We were not created to struggle.

Education became my focus. According to my research, if I went to college I would find a good job and make good money. My classmates in graduate school were married college graduates with decent jobs, yet they continued to struggle financially. I had upgraded my car, moved into my first home and finally received double digit hour pay. At this rate, I still qualified for some food stamps and was allowed to keep my housing voucher if I paid a higher portion of the monthly rent. My classmates and I were working toward establishing professional careers and much higher salaries. I knew that my life would change for the better once I increased my income. At this rate, I could potentially double or triple my income post Masters graduation. In order to reach my goal, we were going to have to make major sacrifices.

No TV, no cable, sleeping on the couch instead of purchasing a new bed, no eating out, no vacations, no hanging out except birthdays—sometimes—and no dating. My desire to cross over allowed me to maintain my radical actions and sacrifices. Intuitively I knew that I had to give up or delay parts of my life to climb to the next level. As a twenty-something I desired love, affection and intimacy. The fear of allowing someone into my life scared me. I didn't want or need to slow down. Relationships require time and effort and I had none to spare. I watched my peers marry and have children as I collected degrees, professional licenses and certifications. "It can wait", I told myself. Too many people were investing in love and relationships but very little into themselves or children. I needed more! I had watched couples struggle together, fail together and win together but it wasn't worth the risk for me.

Love and relationships meant risk. It meant potentially getting distracted and never accomplishing my goals. Love meant depending on someone to be loyal and trustworthy. Relationships meant spending time and money on someone when I barely had enough for myself. Relationships and marriage correlated with heartbreak, betrayal, deceit, abuse, anger, pain, resentment, fights, arguments. It wasn't worth it and I refused to risk losing my momentum. Deep inside I longed to show my children a healthy, loving relationship. "One day", I promised myself.

Creating new traditions, doing something different, stepping out into the unknown is never easy. Poverty is both a reality and mentality. Growing up around my grandparents was a blessing.

Being exposed to poverty was part of my journey. Becoming a teenage mother, dropping out of high school, being victim of domestic violence, childhood illness; it was all part of my story and each aspect exposed me to many trials and taught me valuable lessons about life and overcoming. I learned something about myself: I am a warrior, fighter, and survivor. I face life battles with a silent courage. I break down barriers outside of myself and within myself. I've broken the cycle.

CHAPTER 8: HEALING

Headaches, blurred vision, weight loss, difficulty falling asleep, decreased appetite, irritable, difficulty concentrating and controlling worry. My new doctor prescribed Prozac and encouraged me to seek professional counseling to address the root cause of my Anxiety Disorder. My eye twitched for weeks and I became so dizzy while driving on the highway that I had to pull over immediately. Those were the signs that I needed to get help; the stress was showing up in my physical health.

I've diagnosed thousands of clients with mental health and addiction disorders and yet here I was with a mental health diagnosis and prescription. I instantly related to the feelings of embarrassment and confusion my clients must have felt. Interestingly, I felt a sense of relief. Finally, I was being forced to come to terms with my reality and take care of myself. Two months earlier my world seem to fall apart. I totaled my car in a three-way collision, my grandfather was diagnosed with Kidney Failure, and my children and I were displaced from our home due to water damage. My anxiety flared most often at work around my supervisor. Her presence triggered my perfectionistic side and I worried about losing my job and not being able to provide for my children. I worried about everything! Being homeless, paying bills, getting sick, my grandparent's health, my brother's well-being, my children, passing licensure exams, career goals, gaining weight; I constantly worried.

The Prozac caused extreme drowsiness initially but at least I was finally able to sleep. The interesting thing about slowing down my thoughts was my ability to now focus. The fleeting thoughts had been my safe-haven because I did not have to face them. Now, I was able to both acknowledge my thoughts and confront them. How do I really feel about myself, my life and my future? What happened to me? How has what happened to me affected who I am as a woman and mother? I was a victim. My parents should have never exposed me to their physical nor verbal altercations. It was not my responsibility to save my mother, to be her listening ear, nor to co-parent with her. It was not my responsibility to watch over my brothers and attempt to protect them from older boys. It was not my responsibility to stay awake all night waiting for my mother to arrive home from night clubs. It was not fair to be subjected to the various men in and out of our home and their sexual encounters with my mother. It was not fair to me to learn to be mistrustful of other females because of my mother's experiences. It was not fair that I was taught money is associated with love.

The resentment lingered and I realized that I was angry toward the men in my life. Where were you when I needed protection? I needed protection. No longer am I afraid to ask the questions: Dad, where were you when I was a little girl? Did you fight to be in our lives despite the ridged relationship between you and my mother? What happened to our talk about boys and how beautiful I am? I needed that! Where were you when my brothers began to struggle in school and gained those negative labels? Why didn't you sign them up for sports to give them something positive to do? Why did you leave my mother to struggle financially to raise your first three children? Why didn't you intervene before my brothers were placed in multiple group homes? Why didn't you intervene when my brother began having sex too early with various girls and producing multiple babies? Where were you?

Anger lingered too. Resentment and anger somehow became intertwined and I was lost within those emotions. My entire life was shaped by decisions made as a teenager. My opportunity to travel, to explore multiple career options, the freedom to leave wherever I desired, the ability to splurge on myself; I lost it all. I watched my mother struggle as a young woman with three children; I never desired that for myself. I remember the expression of frustration on her face as she screamed, "I wish ya'll would just run away!" We felt as though we destroyed her opportunity to live a life of freedom. Although she attempted to hide her dismay at times, it became more obvious. How do my children view me as a mother? Do they think I view them as mistakes or barriers to my success? If I could change the trajectory of my life, would I do life without kids?

The lack of sleep, financial support or time to myself increased my resentment and anger toward their father. I was left scraping pennies together to make ends meet while he enjoyed traveling across the country, dating, wearing expensive clothing and driving luxury cars. I wanted a Mercedes and Range Rover too! Why was life so unfair that I was forced to work hard and spend my earnings on our children while he still had the freedom to choose? He took my freedom away. Why did he hurt me physically, emotionally, verbally and sexually when all I gave was loyalty and love? What do I do with the scars? Why did he create yet another single parent home and leave my children without a father? When women become victims of abuse we lose our sense of power and control. For many years, I flinched whenever a man raised his voice in my presence. On the outside, I presented myself as a strong Black woman but on the inside I felt fragile, empty and vulnerable. I needed to find my true self.

In counseling, I confronted my areas of weakness and dysfunctional thinking. I'd learned over the years to mistrust others. I felt a sense of powerlessness after enduring partner rape. I feared raising children alone without guidance. I reasoned with my parent's actions and learned to forgive. I explored my unrealistic fears and anxieties regarding life goals and aspirations. My unrealistic expectations of myself stemmed from my striving to coping with the chaos in which I lived with for many years. My entire thought process was rewired. I was finally free to take care of myself, accept myself, love myself and teach others how to do the same. As I unpacked my baggage, I came face to face with memories and past experiences hidden deep within my subconscious. I went to war with my old self to save the child I was, forgive my teenage self and to release the woman I was to become. My healing is an ongoing process and the journey.

www.ingramcontent.com/pod-product-compliance
Lightning Source LLC
Chambersburg PA
CBHW052116070526
44584CB00017B/2503